YOU'RE SPECIAL

A GUIDE TO POSITIVE SELF ESTEEM AND EXCEPTIONAL LIVING

RALPH SEGUN DADA

YOU'RE SPECIAL

A GUIDE TO POSITIVE SELF ESTEEM AND EXCEPTIONAL LIVING

RALPH SEGUN DADA

Published by:
WOW GLOBAL RESOURCES LIMITED.
IKOSI, LAGOS NIGERIA.
Phone no: 234-8075170325,
Email: wowglobals@gmail.com,
ralphsegundada@gmail.com

ISBN: 978-978-957-014-0

Cover design by:
Samuel Awoma
awomasamuel@gmail.com

Book Packaged by:
Gracehouse Publishing
08138643529

DEDICATION

This book is dedicated to all the people who desire to live a life full of joy and confidence and be sufficient with their outstanding personality, regardless of people's opinions that may seem to limit their exceptional nature.

"Those that don't celebrate their unique identity always lose their originality"

Ralph Segun Dada (RSD).

CONTENTS

PRAISES FOR YOU'RE SPECIAL

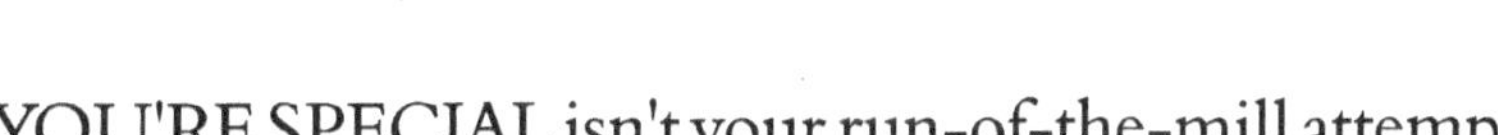

YOU'RE SPECIAL isn't your run-of-the-mill attempt at helping people discover their identity.

In this book, Pastor Ralph Segun Dada has created a manual that will help people refocus on what's most important in order to truly discover themselves.

I can absolutely relate with several aspects of the book as it is a reminder that my identity isn't based on people's opinions, expectations or even the sometimes, unhealthy demands I place on myself but on who God has called me to be.

Social media, unfortunately, can put a lot of pressure on people who don't understand who they are, as they easily compare their lives with carefully selected images posted on these platforms.

I therefore recommend YOU'RE SPECIAL to everyone, not just people struggling with personal identity crisis, to remind us that we're unique and created for a special purpose, incomparable to anyone else's. I gifted 30 copies of this amazing book to my team members and I see a huge improvement in the lives of those who have been reading their copies. They walk and talk with such confidence now than ever before and I can't wait to see a total transformation in their lives.

VICTORIA SAMSON
Media Professional.

Ralph Segun Dada's latest book, YOU'RE SPECIAL, raises the DNA question as it touches on that core, albeit defining factor in the life of every man and woman - IDENTITY. Whatever he does or fails to do - whatever he feels capable or incapable of doing or becoming - is a reflection of his grasp of the identity question and Segun Dada espouses this relevance in a breezy, easy to understand manner.

KINGSLEY OBOM-EGBULEM
Teens / Parenting Counselor.
Author, When Fishes Climb Trees

Drawing inspiration from the word of God, the central theme of the book YOU'RE SPECIAL is our uniqueness as individuals. Simply put, God broke the mold after He made each one of us; we were not mass produced. This understanding should give us a positive image of ourselves and make no room for any uncertainty about who we are.

Personal identity, how you see yourself, is often shaped by early experiences in life. Discovering who you truly are in God is a breakthrough which usually takes a process. This book by R. Segun Dada is practical and could be a good start to that process.

Pastor Ralph Segun Dada opens the readers' eyes to the power of their individuality and uniqueness in a simple to read practical style. YOU'RE SPECIAL will inspire you to embrace your future with confidence and your past without regrets. You are unique in your wiring. Don't let anyone or anything tell you otherwise.

You would love this book!

FOLAKE ODEDIRAN
Country Chair, Sanofi (Nigeria & Ghana).

In this book, Pastor Ralph Segun Dada has revealed the secrets of personal identity to provoke personal Productivity. No man has an excuse not to be productive - find who you are, why you are here and give the world your best shot of what you 'uniquely' carry!

I recommend this book to anyone who is thinking of how to find who they really are, anyone who is doubting what they are here on earth to do, anyone who is asking what capacity they have to create an impact on earth! Read it and apply all the principles. Your productivity will be proof of your identity discovery!

REMI DAIRO
President, Institute of Productivity and Business Innovation Management (IPBIM)

We all come pre-packaged with uniqueness. Unwrapping this unique package called YOU cannot be done without an understanding of your identity and why you were sent here. Ralph Segun Dada (RSD) encapsulated this critical quest in this well-written guide to a healthy self esteem and how to maximize your unique personality.

As you embark on this journey to discovery, may you arrive at the realisation of your highest self. May you find the push to fufil your purpose in making this world more colourful- because you discovered and released yourself.

BOYE OLOYEDE
Innovation Strategist, Coach and Associate Pastor, Daystar Christian Centre

FEEDBACK FROM READERS

I gave copies of YOU'RE SPECIAL to my kids and few other young people around me. They all have wonderful things to say as to how the book has been a blessing to them. My god-daughter in particular says the book has helped her greatly in dealing with her esteem issues and generally, she's having a better relationship with her colleagues at work as a result of reading the book. She's had the book for less than one week! We're thankful to God for His work through you and trust that His grace will continue to flourish in and through you. God bless you plentifully sir.

COLLINS OLA

The book YOU ARE SPECIAL by Ralph Segun Dada is a revalidation of who we are, whose we are and what we are made of. The book has a calming effect like the still waters the Psalmist described in Psalm 23. It also comes with plenty of rhymes and mantras to chant when depression comes calling. I have nicknamed it the "oasis of bliss". It's a must read for everyone and anyone on the road to self-discovery and recovery.

FLOURISH KOLA

YOU'RE SPECIAL has helped me in this downtime. I'm glad I found some new truths in the book that I haven't read elsewhere. I feel really special having read the book. The last chapter and that which spoke about proximity were my favorite. God bless the writer.

MAGRET THOMAS

The book is amazing! It has given me a totally new perspective on God's love for me. Now I understand that God birthed us; we are His children. I mean God literally gave birth to us and loves us tenderly. Even though we rebelled, His love is far-reaching. He is endlessly coming after us.

I was really intrigued with the breakdown of people's makeup in the first chapter. I used to consider some temperaments as weak - as far as I was concerned, the melancholy was superior. But after reading the book, there was a complete shift in my understanding of people's makeup. God intentionally made some people sanguine, melancholy, phlegmatic and others choleric because He has uses for the different expressions of the personalities to accomplish what He intends. If all people were Melancholy, nothing would be done. I can't even begin to talk about posterity - lineage. It's amazing how, even though I have been brought into a new lineage, I stayed stuck in the earthly one. I am essentially of God and from God, nothing beats that!

Then to my favorite part of the book - PROXIMITY. Oh, the love of God! My heart leaps for joy just at the thought of it! Don't get me wrong. Every part of this beautiful piece is, of a truth, mind blowing. Depending on what your current realities are, some truths just hit you harder in some areas because they deal with issues that are personal to you.

Whether you're going through a downtime or just wondering if God truly loves you, this book is a must read. Trust me, at the end of this book, joy will fill your heart again.

Thanks RSD, for sharing these amazing truths with the world. Looking forward to reading more from you. God abundantly bless you. You will fulfill your purpose and calling. Please keep writing. The world needs this!

GLORY EMMANUEL

The book YOU ARE SPECIAL reaffirms my inner convictions that I have all it takes to prosper. Self-Knowledge + Personal Relational Knowledge of God + Active Imaginative Power - all create within me yearnings for more from life. The first chapter especially got me excited when at a point in there, I saw a vivid description of ME! That excitement translated into the willingness to rearrange my priorities while giving me a motivational boost to pursue all that matters to me. The realization of my uniqueness creates in me the persistence to BECOME... A wholesome therapy on Success it is!

MODUPE PETER

Everyone should read 'You re Special'. Thanks for demystifying the myth surrounding what makes an individual special. I was caught a little unawares thou - most of the things I saw in the book I had barely heard in your teachings.

JOY FAVOUR

My life has taken a new dimension and assumed a higher level of meaning by my encounter with this masterpiece. I recommend it infinitely to anyone who is truly LIVING.

KING OGBE

Thanks for the book. Just today, I was caught in a situation that made me feel inferior but YOU'RE SPECIAL reminded me of how truly special I am.

JAMES OKPALA

Thanks for writing this amazing piece. It was indeed an inspiration - best book I have read this year. Indeed I am special!

FATIMA LATIF

INTRODUCTION

YOU'RE SPECIAL is a series of thought provoking principles that will help any individual to perfectly deal with the greatest battle of life which is '*the battle of identity*'. A lot of people have lost their self-esteem, confidence and character to the battle of identity.

"Lack of proper personal identity is the reason most people live in mediocrity, depravity, instability, infidelity, insecurity, hostility, insincerity, and end up as a nonentity" RSD.

However, the principles in this little piece will help any individual build a pleasant and peaceful personality for satisfactory living.

> *But YOU'RE SPECIAL: a kingdom of priests, a holy nation. "This is what I want you to tell the People of Israel.*[1]

God told Moses to emphasize to His people that they are very special to Him. This is because people need a good self-esteem and identity to be able to exhibit outstanding capacity. This little piece in your hand was inspired to boost your ability as well as enhance your dignity so that you can develop a healthy personality that will enhance the optimal fulfillment of your dreams, visions and goals regardless of the difficulty or challenge you may encounter in life.

Thanks a million for showing interest in this book. Have a pleasant experience with it.

Ralph Segun Dada (RSD).

www.ralphsegundada.com

You can connect with Ralph by following him on his social media handles

@rsegundada

@rsegundada

@rsegundada

@rsegundada

Subscribe to Ralph Segun Dada
RSDTV On Youtube

PERSONALITY

"A healthy personality comes from the right understanding of your identity." – RSD

One of the greatest battles you will ever fight in life is the battle of IDENTITY. Lack of a proper understanding of identity is the reason many people are living their lives without joy, satisfaction and a sense of fulfillment. This is in spite of their large material possessions, professions and high connections.

The world is filled with people who compare themselves with others in everything. There are those who love to compete with others as well as those who complain about other people because they are different from them either because of the way they look or the way they do things. Sometimes, people find themselves criticizing others because they hold divergent perspectives on certain issues. One of the reasons people condemn themselves, have low self-esteem and eventually go into depression is their inability to discover, appreciate and embrace the reality of their uniqueness. God created every man to be unique and special.

The fact that no two people have the same finger print, heartbeat, voice tone and so on lends credence to our uniqueness. And our difference is deliberate; it is not a mistake. Perhaps you do not really appreciate your uniqueness. Let me try and help you understand that you are not inferior to anyone and no one is better than you. You are the very best of yourself. You only need to place great value on your personality, gifts, talents and abilities and maximize them to the fullest. Never envy others because of who they are, what they have, where they are and what they have accomplished or achieved in life. The truth is, we all have equal capacity to attain our full potentials and fulfill our purpose in life.

However, an in-depth understanding of our unique personality is fundamental to living a confident, satisfied and peaceful life regardless of what people say about us or how we feel about ourselves based on our personality traits and make up.

Some people are **Sanguine**. They are warm, lively, fun-loving, compassionate, optimistic, friendly and very out-spoken by nature. A typical example is Peter in the bible. In the Gospels, he was portrayed as someone that loved to talk about anything. For instance he was the one that asked Jesus what their gain would be after leaving all their achievements to follow Him:

> *Then Peter said to him, "We left everything to follow you. What will we get out of it?" And Jesus replied, "When I, the Messiah, shall sit upon my glorious throne in the Kingdom, you my disciples shall certainly sit on twelve thrones judging the twelve tribes of Israel. And anyone who gives up his home, brothers, sisters, father, mother, wife, children, or property, to follow me, shall receive a hundred times as much in return, and shall have eternal life."*[2a]

Some people, like Peter, are very bold, inquisitive and would freely express themselves regardless of the status of who they are communing with. Such people should not be perceived as disrespectful or too forward but simply as distinct and forward looking. If Peter could ask Jesus that question, let no one intimidate you out of asking any question that you seek clarity on. People with this personality usually make excellent sales and marketing personnels, travel agents, fashion lovers, cooks, sports lovers, great actors, entertainers, preachers (particularly evangclists) and sometimes teachers. Martha, Mary's sister, can be described as a sanguine because of her boldness and eloquence. She freely expressed and reported to Jesus, her displeasure at the fact that her sister left her to cater for the people alone. It was the same Martha that told Jesus, when He was about to raise Lazarus, their brother, who had been dead for four days, not to bother because he would have been stinking. Jesus didn't rebuke or condemn her for her outspoken nature. Rather, He encouraged her in love so she could be her best as well as enjoy God's best for her life.

The people with **Phlegmatic** personality type are usually quiet and a people person. They focus more on harmony and close relationships. They tend to be very loyal spouses/workers as well as loving parents and are extremely dependable. Relationships matter a lot to them. They can get along with people and build solid friendship. They relate well with distant family members and neighbors. People with phlegmatic temperament tend to avoid conflicts and always try to mediate between others to restore peace and harmony. They are very diplomatic and don't like to hurt people which makes them good team members. They can be very organized and work well under pressure. Abraham in the bible can be described as a phlegmatic. He was a peace loving man. He allowed his nephew to choose the best part of the land before him and even heeded his wife's advice at his own detriment. At one time, he earnestly pleaded to God for the salvation of a rebellious nation. People with phlegmatic personality type can be very passionate about charity and helping others. They can also do well in careers like nursing, teaching, psychology or counseling, child development and social services.

People with **Choleric** personality type are very savvy, analytical, logical goal-oriented, quick, strong willed, hot and active. They can be very practical. They have the capacity and ability to do well in sales and teaching but essentially in practical subject: politics, military service, sports, and many other active endeavors. Most entrepreneurs and founders of organizations are Cholerics. Apostle Paul was a Choleric, a very zealous Pharisee and persecutor of the early church before he was saved. He pioneered the early church in several cities and nations through his missionary trips. Even when he was warned not to go to some places because of the tribulations he would encounter there, he still went because he had a will power that defied any form of opposition. People with this personality are often confrontational and love to prove their points and win over arguments.

People with **Melancholic** personality type are easy going and have traditional mindset. Such are systematic, organized, groomed, neat, structured, detailed, accurate and specific. Melancholies usually love to sacrifice for others. They are creative, intelligent and possess a very good ability for dreaming and imagination. They love loneliness and thrive in it. They are very sensitive, perfectionist, faithful friends and lovers. They are very good people managers. They do well in careers like management, accounting, social work and administration. A very large number of the world's famous and outstanding composers, artists, musicians, inventors, philosophers, theoreticians, theologians, scientists, and devoted educators have been predominantly Melancholies. John the Apostle was a melancholy. This is reflected in his depth of love for God and people. He was banished to a lonely Island and yet was strong enough to document great revelations from God after several attacks and persecutions.

All these personalities have their unique strengths and weaknesses. Hence, none should be regarded as better than the other because each has been designed by God for specific purposes and plans. Therefore, no one is superior or inferior to another. As an individual, your personality is just appropriate for the accomplishment of God's plans for your life. A further study of these sixteen different personality types would enhance your understanding of your personality for an outstanding life.

DESCRIPTION OF SIXTEEN PERSONALITY TYPES

1. **ISTJ (Introverted Sensing Thinking Judging) Introverted Thinking with Extraverted Thinking. The Duty Fulfiller:** Serious and quiet, interested in security and peaceful living. Extremely thorough, responsible, and dependable. Well-developed powers of concentration. Usually

interested in supporting and promoting traditions and establishments. Well-organized and hardworking, they work steadily towards identified goals. They can usually accomplish any task once they have set their mind to it.

2. **ISTP (Introverted Sensing Thinking Perceiving) Introverted Thinking with Extraverted Sensing. The Mechanic**: Quiet and reserved, interested in how and why things work. Excellent skills with mechanical things. They are Risk-takers too .Usually interested in and talented at extreme sports. Uncomplicated in their desires. Loyal to their peers and to their internal value systems, but not overly concerned with respecting laws and rules if they get in the way of getting something done. Detached and analytical, they excel at finding solutions to practical problems.

3. **ISFJ (Introverted Sensing Feeling Judging) Introverted Sensing with Extraverted Feeling. The Nurturer**: Quiet, kind, and conscientious. Can be depended on to follow through. Usually puts the needs of others above their own needs. Stable and practical, they value security and traditions. Well-developed sense of space and function. Rich inner world of observations about people. Extremely perceptive of other's feelings. Interested in serving others.

4. **ISFP (Introverted Sensing Feeling Perceiving) Introverted Feeling with Extraverted Sensing. The Artist:** Quiet, serious, sensitive and kind. Does not like conflict, and is not likely to do things which may generate conflict. Loyal and faithful. Extremely well-developed senses and aesthetic appreciation for beauty. Not interested in leading or controlling others. Flexible and open-minded. Likely to be original and creative. Enjoy the present moment.

5. **INFJ (Introverted intuitive Feeling Judging) Introverted Intuition with Extraverted Feeling. The Protector:** Quietly forceful, original, and sensitive. Tend to stick to things until they are done. Extremely intuitive about people, and concerned for their feelings. Well-developed value systems which they strictly adhere to. Well-respected for their perseverance in doing the right thing. Likely to be individualistic, rather than leading or following.

6. **INFP (Introverted Intuitive Feeling Perceiving) Introverted Feeling with Extraverted Intuition. The Idealist**: Quiet, reflective, and idealistic. Interested in serving humanity. Well-developed value system, which they strive to live in accordance with. Extremely loyal. Adaptable and laid-back unless a strongly-

held value is threatened. Usually talented writers. Mentally quick, and able to see possibilities. Interested in understanding and helping people.

7. **INTJ (Introverted Intuitive Thinking Judging) Introverted Intuition with Extraverted Thinking. The Scientist:** Independent, original, analytical, and determined. Have an exceptional ability to turn theories into solid plans of action. Highly value knowledge, competence, and structure. Driven to derive meaning from their visions. Long-range thinkers. Have very high standards for their performance, and the performance of others. Natural leaders, but will follow if they trust existing leaders.

8. **INTP (Introverted Intuitive Thinking Perceiving) Introverted Thinking with Extraverted Intuition. The Thinker:** Logical, original, creative thinkers. Can become very excited about theories and ideas. Exceptionally capable and driven to turn theories into clear understandings. Highly value knowledge, competence and logic. Quiet and reserved, hard to get to know well. Individualistic, having no interest in leading or following others.

9. **ESTP (Extraverted Sensing Thinking Perceiving) Extraverted Sensing with Introverted Thinking. The Doer:** Friendly,

adaptable, action-oriented. "Doers" who are focused on immediate results. Living in the here-and-now, they're risk-takers who live fast-paced lifestyles. Impatient with long explanations. Extremely loyal to their peers, but not usually respectful of laws and rules if they get in the way of getting things done. Great people skills.

10. **ESTJ (Extraverted Sensing Thinking Judging) Extraverted Thinking with Introverted Sensing) The Guardian:** Practical, traditional, and organized. Likely to be athletic. Not interested in theory or abstraction unless they see the practical application. Have clear visions of the way things should be. Loyal and hard-working. Like to be in charge. Exceptionally capable in organizing and running activities. "Good citizens" who value security and peaceful living.

11. **ESFP (Extraverted Sensing Feeling Perceiving) Extraverted Sensing with Introverted Feeling. The Performer:** People-oriented and fun-loving; they make things more fun for others by their enjoyment. Living for the moment; they love new experiences. They dislike theory and impersonal analysis. Interested in serving others. Likely to be the center of attention in social situations. Well-developed common sense and practical ability.

12. **ESFJ (Extraverted Sensing Feeling Judging) Extraverted Feeling with Introverted Sensing. The Caregiver:** Warm-hearted, popular, and conscientious. Tend to put the needs of others over their own needs. Feel strong sense of responsibility and duty. Value traditions and security. Interested in serving others. Need positive reinforcement to feel good about themselves. Well-developed sense of space and function.

13. **ENFP (Extraverted Intuitive Feeling Perceiving) Extraverted Intuition with Introverted Feeling. The Inspirer:** Enthusiastic, idealistic, and creative. Able to do almost anything that interests them. Great people skills. Need to live life in accordance with their inner values. Excited by new ideas, but bored with details. Open-minded and flexible, with a broad range of interests and abilities.

14. **ENFJ (Extraverted Intuitive Feeling Judging) Extraverted Feeling with Introverted Intuition. The Giver**: Popular and sensitive, with outstanding people skills. Externally focused, with real concern for how others think and feel. Usually dislike being alone. They see everything from the human angle, and dislike impersonal analysis. Very effective at managing people issues, and leading group discussions. Interested in serving others, and

probably place the needs of others over their own needs.

15. **ENTP (Extraverted Intuitive Thinking Perceiving) Extraverted Intuition with Introverted Thinking. The Visionary:** Creative, resourceful, and intellectually quick. Good at a broad range of things. Enjoy debating issues, and may be into "one-up-manship". They get very excited about new ideas and projects, but may neglect the more routine aspects of life. Generally outspoken and assertive. They enjoy people and are stimulating company. Excellent ability to understand concepts and apply logic to find solutions.

16. **ENTJ (Extraverted Intuitive Thinking Judging) Extraverted Thinking with Introverted Intuition. The Executive:** Assertive and outspoken - they are driven to lead. Excellent ability to understand difficult organizational problems and create solid solutions. Intelligent and well-informed, they usually excel at public speaking. They value knowledge and competence, and usually have little patience with inefficiency or disorganization.[2b]

It is vital that you appreciate your personality type and never allow anyone, institution, cultures or opinions of people to undermine your personality. You must in turn accept and appreciate all other personality types. Our ability to accept and celebrate our own distinct personality as well as embrace that of others is what makes our world a better place. We must accept and appreciate people's different personality types just like we accept the different parts of our body without critiquing any part of it. Imagine what we would look like if our entire body comprised only of a head without hands, feet, heart and other organs in the body. Just like our different body parts are suited for their functions, so are the personality types of people perfect for their unique purposes and assignments on earth.

"Never allow anyone make you think that you are too weak or too weird because of your personality type. No, you're not! It is just that you are created and wired to function differently from other people on earth. You are simply special!" - **RSD**

Accept and appreciate who you are regardless of whether other people accept and appreciate you or not, because you are uniquely designed by God for your special purpose. Don't allow the prejudice of people that you are too slow, sharp, eloquent and so on make you lose your peculiar flavor. Learn to say, like David, that you are uniquely made by God.

> *You formed **the way I think and feel**. You put me together in my mother's womb. I praise you because you made me in*

> *such a wonderful way. I know how amazing that was!*
>
> *You made my whole being; you formed me in my mother's body. I praise you because* ***you made me in an amazing and wonderful way. What you have done is wonderful. I know this very well.***
>
> *You made all the delicate, inner parts of my body and knit them together in my mother's womb.* ***Thank you for making me so wonderfully complex!*** *It is amazing to think about. Your workmanship is marvelous-and how well I know it.*[2c]

Avoid the trap of allowing people compare you with themselves or comparing yourself with others. It is the easiest way to lose your originality in life. The best version of another person you can be is a duplicate but what the world eagerly awaits is your original. If you're ever tempted to compare yourself with people or you find people comparing themselves with you for any reason, just remember the wisdom from Paul:

> ***We do not dare to classify or compare ourselves with some who commend themselves. When they measure themselves by themselves and compare themselves with themselves, they are not wise.***
>
> *We're not, understand, putting ourselves in a league with those who boast that they're our superiors.* ***We wouldn't dare do that. But in all this comparing and grading***

and competing, they quite miss the point.

Not that we [have the audacity to] venture to class or [even to] compare ourselves with some who exalt and furnish testimonials for themselves! However, ***when they measure themselves with themselves and compare themselves with one another, they are without understanding and behave unwisely.***[2d]

But you are a chosen race, a royal priesthood, a dedicated nation; [God's] own purchased, SPECIAL PEOPLE, *that you may set forth the wonderful deeds and display the virtues and perfections of Him Who called you out of darkness into His marvelous light.*[2e]

"You cannot build a healthy personality or exhibit unusual abilities without an awareness of your identity."

- RSD

What were your key learning points from this chapter?

What are the new things you will do or actions you will take with these lessons?

PECULIARITY

"If God made you master over all creatures except your fellow man, then you matter in any association, organization or nation you might find yourself." RSD

In the first part of this book, we focused on your identity and we concluded that when you have a good understanding of your identity, you are bound to have a healthy PERSONALITY. In other words, you will be free from the troubles and anxieties that afflict the people who lack an adequate understanding of their unique personality.

Our focus in this chapter will be on YOUR PECULIARITY. Peculiarity, according to the web dictionary means "distinguishing traits" and one of the synonyms is SPECIALNESS. You're peculiar simply because, among all of God's creations, none was made uniquely like you. The Bible tells us that God spoke all other creatures into existence but when it came to creating man, not only did He speak, He also made man in His own image and likeness.

As a man (or woman) you belong to the class that God considers special. This implies that you are more valuable than, and incomparable to everything else in the world. From the story in Genesis, it is very clear that Adam was separated from other creatures. Even though he was the last to be created, yet he was given power over all other creatures. More specifically, he was given the power and prerogative to name them as he desired. You have the same power today. Therefore, don't ever allow anyone, challenge, or circumstance define you because you are designed to call things whatever name you please. When you go through issues, you have the authority to call them what you want because you are SPECIAL.

> *Then God said, "Let us make a man - someone like ourselves, to be the master of all life upon the earth and in the skies and in the seas".*[3a]

When you have a good grasp of your peculiarity, you will be free from the hatred and animosity that some people display towards others especially those who appear to be different from them. You will also live a life of simplicity and approach life issues peaceably. The story of Joseph and his brothers is remarkable and replete with lessons on confidence, contentment, the need to live a life devoid of envy for what others have and the place of rugged courage in the strive to overcome life's negative circumstances. Joseph's brothers envied him to the point where it degenerated to hatred.

> *And the patriarchs [Jacob's sons],* ***boiling with envy and hatred and anger,*** *sold Joseph into slavery in Egypt; but God was with him.*[3b]

Can you imagine what envy could lead to? They didn't understand their own peculiarity. The truth is Joseph identified his peculiar gifts and abilities early on in his life and he was contented with them. The fact that he was the eleventh child of his father didn't bother him. Another person would have worried about whether or not he stood a good chance of getting any substantial inheritance from his father being in that position. Joseph was able to celebrate his peculiarity because he was aware of it. This reference proofs that he was truly peculiar and different from his brothers.

> *The blessings of your father have surpassed the blessings of my ancestors Up to the utmost bound of the everlasting hills;* ***May they be on the head of Joseph, and on the crown of the head of the one DISTINGUISHED among his brothers.***[3c]

Joseph's brothers didn't realize they also had their own unique gifts and talents. They envied Joseph because he had the special ability to dream and interpret dreams.

They also envied his coat of many colors. You don't have to envy anyone's dress when you can dress your own gifts up for global standards and performances. People who make great impact and have outstanding achievements in life are able to do so by first appreciating their gifts and embracing their difference and uniqueness. Bill Gates developed his computer skills, Ronaldo maximized his football skills, Bishop Jakes optimized his preaching skills and Nelson Mandela took his passion for political struggles and human rights activism to an exceptional level.

We must realize as well, that no one's natural endowments or achievements make them better than or greater than us. We all have the potential to impact our world positively in our own little yet unique ways. The tortoise doesn't envy the bird because it flies neither does the elephant envy the monkey because it climbs trees. So, focus on your difference, peculiarity and uniqueness as that is the key to making a unique and remarkable impact in our world.

The reason Jesus was different from every prophet and religious leader that ever lived (and those yet to come) is because He had a unique identity that was free of sin and iniquity.

He related with sinners, yet was not sinful. He couldn't be sinful because He was born of a virgin. In other words, the seed that produced Him wasn't contaminated by the nature of sin that is inherent in man. Humans commit sin because of the nature of sin in us and not because of any culture, circumstances or temptation just the same way a dog barks not because it senses any challenge but because it was designed to bark.

Jesus was conscious of His uniqueness as one with a divine personality, and with that came a wholesome identity despite all the animosity from His persecutors. It was the understanding of His unique nature that motivated Him to confidently say that He is **The Way** to freedom from the sin and iniquity that is ravaging the human race; **The Truth** that can unravel all the lies of the devil that were used to deceive the first man and woman and **The Life** that can quicken every dead situation in your life. I encourage you to maximize your peculiarity and difference so that you can experience significantly different and peculiar results in all your endeavors. Learn from and lean on Jesus for strength and stability that will help you to overcome all of life's challenges, temptations, and sin so that you can truly maximize your peculiarity regardless of any affliction from Satan or negative situations.

What were your key learning points from this chapter?

What are the new things you will do or actions you will take with these lessons?

POSTERITY

"You cannot be living an ordinary life when you are created by an extraordinary God" RSD

In the previous chapter, we established the fact that you are special because of your peculiarity. It is therefore important that you live in the understanding that you are made in the image, likeness, uniqueness, greatness and glory of God so that you don't fall into the trap of comparison and competition which is capable of eroding a person's self-esteem, resulting in negative behaviors and situations.

In this chapter, we will focus on another very important reason why you are special and that is your POSTERITY. You see, you belong to a lineage and your POSTERITY counts. Because you are made in the image and likeness of God, having greatness in your gene is a standard. You have God's nature, so **YOU ARE A BIG DEAL**! Walk in that understanding and let no fear cripple your greatness. Every creature is designed to produce after its kind. A lion will give birth to another lion. A dog will produce another dog, and an elephant will produce another elephant. It is absolutely impossible for an elephant to produce a miniature animal. The same is applicable to you! You were created in God's image and likeness. That means God's seed is planted in you, and you can never be anything less than GREAT, regardless of your family background, educational qualifications, social connections or nationality.

Do not allow anyone, anything or any circumstance to limit your potentials. You can't be held down by any economic condition, financial status and so on because you are a child of a great God with a great future. Having the seed of God in you connotes that greatness is already factored in your DNA. For instance, the tiny size of a mustard seed does not portend its true identity. Mustard seeds are small and round. The seeds are usually about one to two millimeters in diameter but can reach an average mature height of between six and twenty feet with a twenty-foot spread when planted. What this demonstrates is that it does not matter how small you may think you are in terms of your physical stature, financial status or educational standard, greatness is resident in you nonetheless!

When you truly understand your true identity in God and you remain planted in Him like a mustard seed planted in the soil, your growth and greatness in life will be evident to all. For as long as a seed remains on the shelf, it will remain the way it is, but when it is planted, the potential in that seed begins to unfold. This is very instructive. We are God's seed and we should not try to live our lives depending only on our skills and abilities without being rooted in God. Some people are finding it difficult to excel and enjoy satisfaction in life because they are not deepening their root in God. The word of God encouraged us to be planted in God so that we can flourish in every area of our lives. Please, ensure you get acquainted with these scriptures:

> ***Those who are planted in the house of the Lord Shall flourish in the courts of our God. They shall still bear fruit in old age; they shall be fresh and flourishing,***
>
> *For they are transplanted into the Lord's own garden and are under his personal care. Even in old age they will still produce fruit and be vital and green.*
>
> *Planted in the house of the Lord, they shall flourish in the courts of our God. [Growing in grace] they shall still bring forth fruit in old age; they shall be full of sap [of spiritual vitality] and [rich in the] verdure [of trust, love, and contentment].*[4a]

When you are connected to God, you cannot remain little because God is not little. God is great so greatness is your natural identity too. If you start out with whatever dream God has given to you in a little way and you are very diligent and also offering excellent services with it, you will not remain little. David in the scripture, started small; he was taking care of ordinary sheep but he eventually ended up as king over a whole nation because greatness was in his gene.

> *See,* ***I and the children whom the Lord has given me, are for SIGNS and for WONDERS in*** *Israel from the Lord of armies whose resting place is in Mount Zion.*[4b]

"You cannot be living an ordinary life when you are created by an extraordinary God" - **RSD.**

What were your key learning points from this chapter?

What are the new things you will do or actions you will take with these lessons?

PROSPERITY

"You are empowered by God to live in prosperity and not in austerity regardless of any difficulty." RSD

In the last chapter, we emphasized the fact that God's gene in your lineage is perpetuated in your posterity. This is an assurance that you are by default, designed for greatness. In this chapter, our focus will be on the provisions and resources that God has endowed you with to make you a SPECIAL PERSONALITY. Whatever God has given to you is for your PROSPERITY, your confidence, welfare, well-being, success, growth and such other benefits.

However, be mindful that these gifts are available for your use at different stages of your life. The more you use these gifts, the better and more prosperous you become. God put so much conscious effort into the creation of man that He made ready everything man would ever need before He created him. Know therefore, that you were created for success and significance and not to suffer or merely survive. No matter the circumstance life brings your way, always remember you were not created to be in need, rather you are to meet the needs of others. Never allow scarcity of resources and economic situations control your emotions. Truth is, you are connected to God.

And, as long as you remain connected to God, your life must reflect His goodness.

"People are poor, not because they lack resources but simply because they are not resourceful." - **RSD**

You have a choice, decide wisely! The fact that you temporarily lack some things is no indication that you are not prosperous. Your prosperity is not in your situation or acquisition but in your deep understanding of your solid connection with God. The story of Joseph is very inspiring because he showed us how it is possible for a man not to allow negative situations and experiences affect his attitude and perception of life. He was a captive, yet he lived like a captain. That is why it was recorded about him that:

> *But the Lord was with Joseph, and he [though a slave]* ***was a successful and prosperous man;*** *and he was in the house of his master the Egyptian.*[5a]

Can you imagine a slave being referred to as a successful and prosperous individual? He was bought by his master from his brothers meaning he became but a mere property of his master with the corollary being that, whatever he had also automatically became that of his master. That terrible situation should have affected his identity and personality, yet he maintained a prosperous mindset. He clearly understood that his prosperity was not rooted in any commodity but in his absolute connectivity to God. He was conscious of God's presence with him in spite of his negative situation.

Never allow circumstances to define you. Perhaps you are reading this and you have some financial or material challenges that is negatively affecting your mind and making you feel inadequate, just calm down and draw inspiration from the story of Joseph. If Joseph could still be described as a successful and prosperous person despite the overwhelming challenges he experienced even as a slave, then you are successful and prosperous too, your current status notwithstanding

> ***God blessed them: "PROSPER! Reproduce! Fill Earth! Take Charge! Be responsible for fish in the sea and birds in the air, for every living thing that moves on the face of Earth".*** [5b]

"You are empowered by God to live in prosperity and not in austerity." – **RSD.**

When God created man, He blessed him with divine prosperity to enable him live his life with great peace and serenity. Being blessed means that one has a divine enablement to flourish and enjoy progress in spite of the challenges of life. When anyone depends on God's supernatural capacity to prosper, no situation of life can make such individual to live like a nonentity. Such absolute dependence on God will make any individual overcome the temptation of begging from others to survive. Just depend entirely upon the Lord, and He will supply all your needs because you are very special to Him. This is His utmost desire for you:

> *Beloved, I pray that you may* ***prosper*** *in all things and be in health, just as your soul* ***prospers****.*[5c]

What were your key learning points from this chapter?

What are the new things you will do or actions you will take with these lessons?

POSSIBILITY

"With a possibility mentality, you will overcome any difficulty and also be able to achieve feats that will make you a lifetime celebrity" - RSD

In preceding chapters, we revealed that you are special because of your personality, peculiarity, posterity and prosperity. However, you cannot fully thrive on these factors until you understand and believe in possibilities.

It has been established in previous chapters that God already planned and programmed our lives with enormous resources for PROSPERITY even before our existence on earth. We are His special creature and that is why all we will need as humans were made available before we were created. In this chapter, our focus will be centered on POSSIBILITY mentality.

Man is the only creature that possesses the amazing combination of will and mind power - the ability to think and imagine possibilities to overcome life's challenges.

Think about this:

> *And the Lord said, "Behold, they are one people and they have all one language; and this is only the beginning of what they will do, and now NOTHING they have* ***IMAGINED*** *they can do will be IMPOSSIBLE for them."*[6a]

A situation in Genesis provoked this amazing statement. Mankind embarked on a project that was seemingly impossible to accomplish. How could people have ever imagined that they could construct a tower that would reach into heaven? They started anyway and God actually said it was possible for them to achieve their goal! God had to interrupt the process but only because their project was merely for selfish gratification and not for His glorification. What this suggests is that any project we embark on, no matter how impossible it seems, can be realized if it is centered on glorifying God and if we hold a possibility mentality towards it.

Because God has given man the capacity to learn and be able to do things just like Him, man has been able to invent various solutions to diverse problems in the field of sciences, arts, technology, medicine, etc. This is proof that you and I are very special and we should never allow any negative situation to limit us. In case you have enormous projects staring you in the face and you have begun to doubt if such project could materialize, just relax and draw inspiration from the above scripture and God will empower your mind with solutions on how it could be accomplished.

"With the power of your imagination you can overcome any limitation." – **RSD**

For instance, as you read this book, it is possible you begin to see yourself in environments different from where you are. In your mind, you can overcome lack, sorrow, sicknesses, bareness and so on. In your mind, you can imagine yourself shaking hands with the richest men and women in the world, presidents of countries and whoever it is you aspire to meet. Knowing how special and powerful God made man, the devil always tries to lie to us by planting negative images in our minds to confuse and limit us.

For man to overcome the temptations of the devil and constantly stay positive in his mind, there is a critical need to constantly plug into the mind of the superior being who lived in this world without any thought of evil. The scriptures clearly stated that He did absolute good without any tinge of evil while He was here on earth. Imbibing His mentality will give you capacity to envision the invisible and also dare and accomplish the impossible. This is assurance that you can achieve all your dreams in life.

> *Jesus went everywhere DOING GOOD FOR PEOPLE.*[6b]
>
> *Let this mind be in you, which was also in Christ Jesus.*[7a]

The superior and supernatural mind that was in Christ made Him to accomplish feats that were considered absolutely impossible. He fed multitudes with little resources, healed various terminal diseases, walked on water and even raised the dead. It is quite amazing that most people don't realize the magnitude of their ability and the resources available to them when they have a solid connection with Christ. Making Jesus your Lord goes beyond mere religious exercise; it's a real invitation to live a victorious and glorious life. Kindly connect with Jesus by inviting Him to be the Lord of your life and your life will experience a wondrous transformation. When you do, you will automatically have access to His mental capacity and be able to reason at His frequency. Do meditate on this provision:

> *For who has known or understood the mind (the counsels and purposes) of the Lord so as to guide and instruct Him and give Him knowledge?* ***But we have the mind of Christ (the Messiah) and do hold the thoughts (feelings and purposes) of His heart.***[7b]

Your connection with Christ is your access to His mind. You will be able to think like Him and take on projects like He did. When you function with His possibility mentality, you will be able to overcome any kind of difficulty be it in your health, relationships, businesses and so on. You will be able to dream big dreams, dare great tasks and also accomplish impossible feats. When I made Christ the Lord of my life as a teenager, I started seeing things differently in my mind. Being the last Child in a family of nine and having lost my father at a very tender age, the situation of the family was very appalling because my mother had to depend on the meager funds from her restaurant business to take care of all of us. While I assisted her at the restaurant, I started seeing myself in great places. Most of the things I saw in my mind have become my reality now and I am still seeing greater things today.

"With a possibility mentality, you will overcome any difficulty and also be able to achieve feats that will make you a lifetime celebrity" **RSD**

What were your key learning points from this chapter?

What are the new things you will do or actions you will take with these lessons?

PROPENSITY

"No matter what you are going through or will go through in life, always remember that God loves you personally, passionately, practically and permanently" RSD

What MARVELOUS LOVE the Father has extended to us! Just look at it we're called children of God! That's who we really are. But that is also why the world doesn't recognize us or take us seriously, because it has no idea who he is or what he's up to.[8]

This is the way God put it: "They found grace out in the desert, these people who survived the killing. Israel went out looking for a place to rest, ***met God out looking for them!" God told them, "I've never quit LOVING YOU AND NEVER WILL. EXPECT LOVE, LOVE, AND MORE LOVE!"***[9]

One of the reasons people easily get depressed, oppressed and feel rejected and dejected is that they allow their experiences to affect their moods. Living in a world that is full of problems and negative people, it is inevitable that you would be offended and occasionally have your feelings hurt by people's actions or reactions to you. And this could happen intentionally or unintentionally. People may cheat, malign, defraud or even falsely accuse you. Negative circumstances or issues may arise causing you pain emotionally, financially, psychologically, economically or physically. But you must understand that these are some of the challenges of living in an imperfect world full of imperfect people and situations.

These negative situations cannot and will never affect God's love and affection for you. As a matter of fact, God's love for you is just as real, irreversible and irreplaceable even when your actions are not yet conforming to His standards. The prodigal son's story validates the depth of God's love for us even when we have misbehaved or lived our lives in flagrant disregard of His instructions. The young man forcefully demanded his own inheritance from the father, and subsequently squandered it on frivolous living. Perhaps, he got involved with prostitutes, hooligans, and so on, yet his father accepted him back because his love for him was not depended on how good he was.

According to the Mariam Webster dictionary, **PROPENSITY** means ***a strong natural tendency to do something, an often intense natural inclination or***

preference, a habitual attraction to some activity or thing. The synonyms are: affection, affinity, bent, disposition, and partiality, favor, like, liking, preference, SPECIALTY, PECULIARITY and fondness.

The father of the prodigal son had a 'special affection' for his son - despite his negative disposition such that the elder brother felt that his father was partial in favor of his younger brother. But the truth is that God has the same partial love and affection for all of us. This is the whole story as illustrated by Jesus to the crowd to make them understand the extent of God's love for them and how because of this unquenchable love, He is always willing to accept and not reject them no matter their flaws:

> *Then he said, "There was once a man who had two sons. The younger said to his father, 'Father, I want right now what's coming to me.' "So the father divided the property between them. It wasn't long before the younger son packed his bags and left for a distant country. There, undisciplined and dissipated, he wasted everything he had. After he had gone through all his money, there was a bad famine all through that country and he began to hurt. He signed on with a citizen there who assigned him to his fields to slop the pigs. He was so hungry he would have eaten the corncobs in the pig slop, but no one would give him any. "That brought him to his senses. He said, 'All those farmhands working for my father sit down to three meals a day, and here I am starving to death. I'm going back to my father. I'll*

say to him, Father, I've sinned against God, I've sinned before you; I don't deserve to be called your son. Take me on as a hired hand.' He got right up and went home to his father.

"***When he was still a long way off, his father saw him. His heart pounding, he ran out, embraced him, and kissed him****. The son started his speech: 'Father, I've sinned against God, I've sinned before you; I don't deserve to be called your son ever again.'* "***But the father wasn't listening. He was calling to the servants, 'Quick. Bring a clean set of clothes and dress him. Put the family ring on his finger and sandals on his feet. Then get a grain-fed heifer and roast it. We're going to feast!*** *We're going to have a wonderful time! My son is here given up for dead and now alive! Given up for lost and now found!' And they began to have a wonderful time.*

"All this time his older son was out in the field. When the day's work was done he came in. As he approached the house, he heard the music and dancing. Calling over one of the houseboys, he asked what was going on. He told him, 'Your brother came home. Your father has ordered a feast barbecued beef! because he has him home safe and sound'.

"The older brother stalked off in an angry sulk and refused to join in. His father came out and tried to talk to him, but he wouldn't listen. The son said, 'Look how many years I've stayed here serving you, never giving you one moment

of grief, but have you ever thrown a party for me and my friends? Then this son of yours who has thrown away your money on whores shows up and you go all out with a feast!'

"His father said, 'Son, you don't understand. You're with me all the time and everything that is mine is yours but this is a wonderful time, and we had to celebrate. This brother of yours was dead, and he's alive! He was lost, and he's found!'" [10]

When people have adequate understanding of God's love and affection for their lives, they are able to live a life that is free from frustration, dejection, confusion or depression no matter the situation. That understanding also enables them to live a life that is free from the corruption and contamination present in the world especially through immoral behaviors. More importantly, they are motivated to live in constant celebration in spite of any adverse situation.

"The understanding of God's love and affection for you gives reasons for jubilation even when there is no special occasion" **RSD**

The elder brother didn't have such an understanding. He was waiting for the father to celebrate him when he had all the reasons to celebrate himself.

"The truth is that your disposition cannot change God's eternal love and affection for you, rather it would serve as motivation for your total transformation because you will be free from condemnation." – **RSD**

Propensity is all about making you understand that God's love and affection for you is very personal, peculiar, practical and permanent. **If you understand this, you will not live a licentious lifestyle, doing what you like. Instead, you will be motivated to do what is right**. This was the secret of Joseph's strength. That strength empowered him to reject the seductions from Potiphar's wife for him to commit an immoral act with her. He was very conscious of his father's love for Him. He was mindful of the fact that his father made a special coat for him because he was a special child. But God is our greatest father. It was by this same understanding that Jesus lived an exceptional life on earth. He was never depressed nor was any situation able to frustrate or break Him down emotionally. So, you need to keep it always in mind that you are very special. God told Jesus, "***You are my Son, chosen and marked by my LOVE, pride of my life.***"[11a]

One of the basic reasons Jesus came to earth was to give us a deeper understanding of how to relate with God as a father and not only as a creator. Little wonder He taught His disciples to call God father when praying to Him.

God is interested in our relationship with Him, not in our religious practices. Ponder on these words from Jesus on the subject of prayer:

> *And when you come before God, don't turn that into a theatrical production either. All these people making a regular show out of their prayers, hoping for stardom! Do you think God sits in a box seat? "Here's what I want you to do: Find a quiet, secluded place so you won't be tempted to role-play before God. Just be there as simply and honestly as you can manage. The focus will shift from you to God, and you will begin to sense his grace. "The world is full of so-called prayer warriors who are prayer-ignorant. They're full of formulas and programs and advice, peddling techniques for getting what you want from God. Don't fall for that nonsense. This is your Father you are dealing with, and he knows better than you what you need.* ***WITH A GOD LIKE THIS LOVING YOU****, you can pray very simply. Like this:* ***OUR FATHER IN HEAVEN****, Reveal who you are.*[11b]

Those that have a solid understanding that God is a father do have a better perspective of life's negative situations. They are usually calmer and eventually prosper in all that they do. Your earthly father might have abused and abandoned you or you might even have lost your father at a very tender age like me. Never become bitter because you have a better and capable heavenly father who would take proper care of you and ensure you fulfill your life's visions and dreams in grand style.

Sometimes we experience terrible and difficult situations that make us think and feel that God has forsaken us just like the children of Israel concluded during their ordeal. But we should always remember God is there with us and He is working behind the scenes to bring testimonies out of those test and trials.

> *But Zion said, "I don't get it. God has left me. My Master has forgotten I even exist." "Can a mother forget the infant at her breast, walk away from the baby she bore?* ***But even if mothers forget, I'd never forget you never. Look, I've written your names on the backs of my hands. The walls you're rebuilding are never out of my sight.***
>
> *You are our Father. Abraham and Israel are long dead. They wouldn't know us from Adam.* ***But you're our living Father,*** *our Redeemer, famous from eternity!*[11c]

Apostle Paul had a good understanding of the fatherhood of God so he encouraged the Ephesian Church to recognize that approaching God as a father in prayers is the secret to enjoying His response and ultimate provisions. Meditate on his prayers and you will see the tremendous insights and benefits that come from knowing God as a father.

> *For this reason [seeing the greatness of this plan by which you are built together in Christ],* ***I bow my knees before***

the FATHER of our Lord Jesus Christ, For Whom every family in heaven and on earth is named [THAT FATHER FROM WHOM ALL FATHERHOOD TAKES ITS TITLE AND DERIVES ITS NAME]. *May He grant you out of the rich treasury of His glory to be strengthened and reinforced with mighty power in the inner man by the [Holy] Spirit [Himself indwelling your innermost being and personality. May Christ through your faith [actually] dwell (settle down, abide, make His permanent home) in your hearts!* ***May you be rooted deep in love and founded securely on love, That you may have the power and be strong to apprehend and grasp with all the saints [God's devoted people, the experience of that love] what is the breadth and length and height and depth [of it]; [That you may really come] to know [practically, through experience for yourselves] the love of Christ, which far surpasses mere knowledge [without experience]; that you may be filled [through all your being] unto all the fullness of God*** *[may have the richest measure of the divine Presence, and become a body wholly filled and flooded with God Himself]! Now to Him Who, by (in consequence of) the [action of His] power that is at work within us, is able to [carry out His purpose and] do superabundantly, far over and above all that we [dare] ask or think [infinitely beyond our highest prayers, desires, thoughts, hopes, or dreams].*[11d]

There are enormous benefits to enjoy when we understand that God is our father. Gleaning from the prayers of Paul above, we would be able to comprehend His love for us which will strengthen us in our inner man against any and every adversity of life. We will not merely enjoy God's perpetual presence, we will as a matter of fact, become a carrier of His very presence. We will also experience an abundance of His works in us, through us, with us and for us. Above all, He will always exceed our prayers and requests.

The reason Paul was able to thrive despite all the trials, test and persecutions he experienced during his earthly assignment was simply because he understood the propensity of God's love for him. Can you imagine how a man that was stoned to the point of death, dragged out of the city and left for dead could still rise and continue preaching the gospel without getting discouraged? Paul describes some of the challenges he went through:

> *They say they serve Christ? But I have served him far more! (Have I gone mad to boast like this?) I have worked harder, been put in jail more often, been whipped times without number, and faced death again and again and again. Five different times the Jews gave me their terrible thirty-nine lashes. Three times I was beaten with rods. Once I was stoned. Three times I was shipwrecked. Once I was in the open sea all night and the whole next day. I have traveled many weary miles and have been often in great*

danger from flooded rivers and from robbers and from my own people, the Jews, as well as from the hands of the Gentiles. I have faced grave dangers from mobs in the cities and from death in the deserts and in the stormy seas and from men who claim to be brothers in Christ but are not. I have lived with weariness and pain and sleepless nights. Often I have been hungry and thirsty and have gone without food; often I have shivered with cold, without enough clothing to keep me warm. Then, besides all this, I have the constant worry of how the churches are getting along.[11e]

Paul's understanding of God's love for him was so profound that the negative experiences couldn't demoralize him. He was so motivated that even in prison he was writing letters to people that were free, admonishing them to rejoice in God. Paul's believe and personal understanding of God's love made him a phenomenal personality with great and outstanding impacts that will continue to motivate lives till eternity.

"When you are convinced of God's affection for you, difficult situations can't make you a victim of the negative emotions that make people to live in frustration and depression." – **RSD**

The basis of his victory in all the challenges he encountered in life was simply his comprehension and conviction of the propensity of God's love for him. These statements capture it vividly:

> *Who shall ever separate us from* **Christ's love?** *Shall suffering and affliction and tribulation? Or calamity and distress? Or persecution or hunger or destitution or peril or sword? Even as it is written, "For Thy sake we are put to death all the day long; we are regarded and counted as sheep for the slaughter." Yet amid all these things we are more than conquerors and gain a surpassing victory through Him Who loved us. For I am persuaded beyond doubt (am sure) that neither death nor life, nor angels nor principalities, nor things impending and threatening nor things to come, nor powers, nor height nor depth, nor anything else in all creation will be able to separate us* ***from the love of God which is in Christ Jesus our Lord.***[11f]

John, one of the disciples of Jesus, had such a deep understanding of God's love for him that he went on to describe himself as the disciple whom Jesus loved.

> *One of His disciples,* ***whom Jesus loved*** *[whom He esteemed and delighted in], was reclining [next to Him] on Jesus' bosom.*[11g]

Bibles historians said that he was the only disciple of Christ that enjoyed miraculous preservation from death. Several attempts were made on his life but he escaped each time. After a series of assaults, he was banished to an island where he lived for years, received and documented the book of Revelation before he died a peaceful death at a ripe old age.

"Those that have a conviction of God's love and affection for them usually enjoy His divine protection and preservation from all satanic oppressions and afflictions." - **RSD**

You need to personally and practically comprehend and appreciate the love and affection of God for you. When you are convinced beyond any iota of doubt, you will begin to enjoy His supernatural protection, provision and peace irrespective of the situation and circumstances of your life. Understand that though God has a general love for all the people He created, yet His love for you as an individual is personal and special. It is also true that if you have a good understanding of God's love for you, you won't fall victim of lust, selfish or sinful gratifications in this world. The scripture below validates this fact:

> *Do not love the world or the things in the world. If anyone loves the world,* ***the love of the Father is not in him***. *For all that is in the world the lust of the flesh, the lust of the eyes, and the pride of life is not of the Father but is of the world.*[11h]

Those that truly understand this dimension of God's love and affection for them are able to maintain their stability in any situation no matter how difficult and negative they may be - for instance, being jilted in a relationship that looks very promising or being neglected or disdained by people. Resting absolutely on God's love protects one from any form of distress. When people deprive you of their love, you can always depend on God's love for you. People's love is often ephemeral. It is fickle and has a high propensity to change as their situations change. But, God's love is eternal and immutable because He cannot change.

People's love is often consciously or unconsciously influenced by some extraneous factors such as beauty, smartness, work ethics, financial or material resources, attitudes (kindness, calmness, patience etc.) and so on. If it happens that you start to fall short of any of these attributes, the likelihood is that they start reducing the quotient or quality of their love for you. But when it comes to God's love for you, it is eternal and doesn't depend on any condition that you have to meet.

The truth is that even if you change, God cannot change His love for you. Your good works cannot earn God's love. This scripture validate this profound truth:

> *For God* ***SO GREATLY LOVED and dearly prized the world that He [even] gave up His only begotten (unique) Son****, so that whoever believes in (trusts in, clings to, relies on) Him shall not perish (come to destruction, be lost) but have eternal (everlasting) life.*[11i]

God didn't wait for any of your good works to show such great and unexplainable love to you. Your good works cannot and will not measure up to His standards and your bad works or behaviors cannot make Him love you less because He demonstrated His love to you when you were still in your mess not considering that you are still going to commit any wrong action against Him or other people. Think about this:

> *But God* ***shows and clearly proves His [own] love for us by the fact that while we were still sinners,*** *Christ (the Messiah, the Anointed One) died for us.*[11j]

When we get a revelation of God's love for us, it will motivate us to behave right even when there are temptations to do wrong.

Those that truly understand the depth, height, width and length of God's love for them are the only ones capable of sharing it with others. When we have this unique knowledge and experience of God's love, we would be able to forgive others in our relationships even when their actions deeply hurt or break our hearts. Some people think that communication is the life of a relationship but really, it is genuine love and affection that sustains any relationship. What is the benefit of communication without the capacity for forgiveness of transgressions?

"It is your comprehension of God's love and affection that helps you to forgive people's transgressions even if their wrong actions were intentional." – **RSD**

Knowing and understanding the propensity of God's love delivers us from all forms of fear and intimidation that may want to crumple our dreams, visions, and ambitions in life or make us lose our self-esteem and confidence. When Adam sinned against God and God came to commune with Him, he hid from God and told Him that he was afraid because he had transgressed His instructions. God doesn't want us to be far from Him even when we fall short of His standards. For instance, parents don't like it when their erring children run or withdraw from them. Rather, they would expect their children to discuss with them and receive their pardon. If as humans, we would extend such unconditional love and affection to our children, in spite of their shortcomings, how much more would God whose love surpasses that of any human. Apostle John who knew and understood God's perfect love wrote to encourage us about how knowing God's love can give us confidence to relate with Him and also help us receive from Him. Please meditate on his insights about God's love:

> *And we know* ***(understand, recognize, are conscious of, by observation and by experience) and believe (adhere to and put faith in and rely on) the love God cherishes for us. God is love, and he who dwells and continues in love dwells and continues in God, and God dwells and continues in Him.*** *In this [union and communion with Him]* ***love is brought to completion and attains perfection with us,*** *that we may have*

confidence for the day of judgment [with assurance and boldness to face Him], because as He is, so are we in this world. ***There is no fear in love [dread does not exist], but full-grown (complete, perfect) love turns fear out of doors and expels every trace of terror! For fear brings with it the thought of punishment and [so] he who is afraid has not reached the full maturity of love [is not yet grown into love's complete perfection].*** *We love Him, because He first loved us.*[11k]

A full comprehension of God's love and affection for us is a great treasure that can give you and me a vital reason to remain cool, calm and collected in life when confronted with various trials and challenges. We can rest, knowing that God is on our side and He is always with us even when everyone and everything seems to be against us. When the devil came to tempt Jesus he didn't remind Him of how dearly beloved He was, he only asked if He was God's son. He knew that reminding Jesus that He was dearly and deeply loved by God would strengthen Him, boost His confidence in God and also motivate Him to comply with God's instruction rather than fall victim of his temptations. But because Jesus knew that He was excellently loved by God, He refused to fall for the temptations of the devil to disobey God's instructions.

After all the people were baptized, Jesus was baptized. As he was praying, the sky opened up and the Holy Spirit, like

> *a dove descending, came down on him. And along with the Spirit, a voice: "You are my Son,* ***CHOSEN AND MARKED BY MY LOVE, PRIDE OF MY LIFE****."*
>
> *For forty wilderness days and nights he was tested by the Devil. He ate nothing during those days, and when the time was up he was hungry. The Devil, playing on his hunger, gave the first test: "Since you're God's Son, command this stone to turn into a loaf of bread."*[111]

I will conclude with the story of Daniel in the bible. It is quite amazing because he was so special that he served under four administrations; he worked with four kings. He was invited to solve great problems in the government because he remained relevant as a solution provider. He was so distinguished that he was made the head of all his contemporaries in the king's duties. His promotion invoked a lot of envy from several people and for that reason, they conspired against him. That eventually led to him being thrown into the Lion's den, yet he was divinely preserved by God. He maintained a very high standard of integrity as a lifestyle because he had a good understanding of God's love for him. These are some records that show that Daniel was greatly loved by God:

> *And [the angel] said to me, O Daniel,* ***you greatly beloved man****, understand the words that I speak to you*

and stand upright, for to you I am now sent. And while he was saying this word to me, I stood up trembling.

Then he said to me, Fear not, Daniel, for from the first day that you set your mind and heart to understand and to humble yourself before your God, your words were heard, and I have come as a consequence of [and in response to] your words.

And he said, ***O man greatly beloved, fear not! Peace be to you! Be strong, yes, be strong. And when he had spoken to me, I was strengthened and said; let my lord speak, for you have strengthened me".*** [11m]

The understanding that you are greatly loved by God will boost your self-esteem and infuse you with great strength when others may seem to be getting weak emotionally, physically and in other areas of their lives. You will be divinely secured from the devil, diseases, disasters, and demonic machinations against your welfare and entire well-being.

Always remember that no matter the situation you may find yourself in, God's love cannot depart from you because you are very special to Him. That is why He gave His best and most precious gift of His son as a sacrifice for your sin and trespasses against Him. Therefore, ensure you are very convinced and conscious of God's love for you. And, beyond anything or anyone else, make it your major focus in life. This will make your life complete and satisfactory.

> ***Guard and keep yourselves in the LOVE OF GOD;*** *expect and patiently wait for the mercy of our Lord Jesus Christ (the Messiah) [which will bring you] unto life eternal.*[11n]

> *Surely or only goodness, mercy, and* ***UNFAILING LOVE shall follow me all the days of my life****, and through the length of my days the house of the Lord [and His presence] shall be my dwelling place.*[11o]

God has determined that His love will constantly be showered on you even when you are intentionally moving away from Him. The truth is that once you realize that His love is ever constant, you will be motivated to remain consistent in your walk with Him. You will also work for Him with integrity and uprightness of heart and acts. David became a man after God's heart not because he was perfectly upright but simply because he perfectly understood God's love for him.

"God's love and affection for you is very special because truly you are really special." – **RSD.**

What were your key learning points from this chapter?

What are the new things you will do or actions you will take with these lessons?

PROXIMITY

"Your proximity to God will give you grace to express your uniqueness regardless of people's disposition to you or the negative situations of life." RSD

In the past you were spiritually dead because of your sins and the things you did against God. Yes, in the past you lived the way the world lives, following the ruler of the evil powers that are above the earth. That same spirit is now working in those who refuse to obey God. In the past, all of us lived like them, trying to please our sinful selves and doing all the things our bodies and minds wanted. We should have suffered God's anger because of the way we were. We were the same as all other people. ***But God's mercy is great, and he loved us very much.*** *Though we were spiritually dead because of the things we did against God, he gave us new life with Christ. You have been saved by God's grace. And he raised us up with Christ and gave us a seat with him in the heavens. He did this for those in Christ Jesus so that for all future time he could show the very great riches of His grace by being kind to us in Christ Jesus.*

> *I mean that you have been saved by grace through believing. You did not save yourselves; it was a gift from God. It was not the result of your own efforts, so you cannot brag about it. God has made us what we are. In Christ Jesus, God made us to do good works, which God planned in advance for us to live our lives doing. You were not born Jewish. You are the people the Jews call "uncircumcised." Those who call you "uncircumcised" call themselves "circumcised." (Their circumcision is only something they themselves do on their bodies.) Remember that in the past you were without Christ. You were not citizens of Israel, and you had no part in the agreements with the promise that God made to his people. You had no hope, and you did not know God.* ***But now in Christ Jesus, you who were far away from God are brought NEAR through the blood of Christ's death.***[12]

Another amazing insight that gives credence to the fact that you are very special is your unique proximity to God. You must understand your proximity to God as your heavenly father, lover and the One who constantly validates and guides you; One whose presence is always with you even though you may not always feel so and cannot physically behold Him. One of the reasons most people feel lonely, depressed and frustrated is that they think that God is very far from them or they don't have a close relationship with Him. They often feel abandoned by God as a result of their sins and misdemeanors. It is quite amazing that when Adam and Eve sinned against God, it was God that went looking for them even while they were hiding from Him. As a matter of fact, they told God that they were naked and He asked, "Who told you that you were naked?" The Bible captured the conversation thus:

> *And they heard the sound of the Lord God walking in the garden in the cool of the day, and Adam and his wife hid themselves from the presence of the Lord God among the trees of the garden. Then the Lord God called to Adam and said to him, Where are you? He said, I heard the sound of You [walking] in the garden, and I was afraid because I was naked; and I hid myself. And He said, who told you that you were naked? Have you eaten of the tree of which I commanded you that you should not eat?*[13]

The whole idea is that man sinned and God, knowing that man had sinned, still kept drawing nearer to him not regarding his shortcomings. As a matter of fact, it wasn't God that pronounced that man was naked; it was a submission that emanated from his own self-condemnation. They hid themselves from God's Presence; it wasn't God who took His presence from them. But that is exactly what sin does. It brings a separation between you and God through condemnation and shame. That is exactly what happens when children disobey their parents. They feel guilty, condemned and hide away even when the parents are willing to pardon and commune with them.

God so loved man that even when they used leaves to cover themselves, He went ahead and clothed them better by using animal skin to cover their nakedness. But symbolically, God was also resolving their spiritual, emotional and psychological nakedness because He had to shed the blood of the animal to get the skin which served as a temporal covering. However, God proffered a permanent solution to that separation in the shedding of Christ's blood. That one time sacrifice permanently mended the dividing wall between man and God and ensured that man will forever have access to God and enjoy constant nearness to Him. The Bible describes God's total solution to man's separation from Him and the provision for unhindered access to Him this way:

> *For Christ (the Messiah) has not entered into a sanctuary made with [human] hands, only a copy and pattern and type of the true one, but [He has entered] into heaven itself, now to appear in the [very] presence of God on our behalf. Nor did He [enter into the heavenly sanctuary to] offer Himself regularly again and again, as the high priest enters the [Holy of] Holies every year with blood not his own. For then would He often have had to suffer [over and over again] since the foundation of the world. But as it now is,* ***He has once for all at the consummation and close of the ages appeared to put away and abolish sin by His sacrifice [of Himself].***[14]

> *In as much then as we have a great High Priest Who has*

[already] ascended and passed through the heavens, Jesus the Son of God; let us hold fast our confession [of faith in Him]. For we do not have a High Priest Who is unable to understand and sympathize and have a shared feeling with our weaknesses and infirmities and liability to the assaults of temptation, but One Who has been tempted in every respect as we are, yet without sinning. Let us then fearlessly and confidently and boldly ***DRAW NEAR to the throne of grace (the throne of God's unmerited favor to us sinners), that we may receive mercy [for our failures] and find grace to help in good time for every need [appropriate help and well-timed help, coming just when we need it].***[15]

God allowed the blood of Jesus to be shed for our sins simply because you and I are very special to Him. When the devil sinned there wasn't any sacrifice for his sin because he wasn't created in the image and likeness of God. But man was made in God's image and he represents God here on earth. This act of God does not suggest that He is prejudiced against angels or the devil but simply underscores the indisputable fact that human beings are very special to Him. But most people don't have this understanding and that is why they allow the devil to use sin to keep them far away from God. By the blood of Jesus, you and I have unhindered access to God's presence.

The price Jesus paid by His death and resurrection gives

us unusual proximity to God and eternal connection to Him despite life's difficulty.

Anytime you fall short of God's standard, be it intentionally through overwhelming temptations or mistakenly through distractions, don't allow the shame of sin put you in condemnation and make you move far away from God. Rather, let the consciousness of your proximity to God draw you closer to Him in repentance and change of attitude. If you allow regrets to make you run from God you will only persist in such error or sin.

"Christ used His death, which is separation from God, to pay the ultimate penalty for sin in order to give us unusual and unhindered connection and proximity to God and dominion over sin and iniquity." – **RSD**

When Jesus was about to give up His Spirit, He cried out, "My God, my God, why have you forsaken me?" because at that period, He took all our sins on Himself and because God cannot behold sin, there was a separation. The scripture captures the event:

> *About three o'clock, Jesus shouted, "Eli, Eli, lama sabachthani?" which means, "My God, my God, why have you forsaken me?"*
>
> *And look!* ***The curtain secluding the Holiest Place in the Temple was split apart from top to bottom****; and the earth shook, and rocks broke, and tombs opened, and many*

godly men and women who had died came back to life again. After Jesus' resurrection, they left the cemetery and went into Jerusalem, and appeared to many people there.[16]

The death of Jesus and His resurrection gave us access to God's presence. The curtain covering the holiest place which only the high priest could access once in a year with a blood sacrifice for all the people was split so that everybody can have unrestricted access.

"As a child of God, the mentality of your proximity with God gives you boldness to reject all forms of iniquity." ~ **RSD.**

Joseph had a good understanding of his proximity with God even when Jesus had not yet died. He bluntly refused to indulge in immoral acts with Potiphar's wife at a time when doing so seemed justifiable and offered the promise of some form of acceptance, emotional pleasures and possibly financial or material favors since he had experienced a lot of rejection, hatred, animosity and difficulties in life. Most people give in to sinful pleasures for some of these reasons. His refusal was motivated by his unwavering understanding of God's closeness to Him.

Joseph was a strikingly handsome man. As time went on, his master's wife became infatuated with Joseph and one day said, "Sleep with me." He wouldn't do it. He said to his master's wife, "Look, with me here, my master doesn't

> *give a second thought to anything that goes on here he's put me in charge of everything he owns. He treats me as an equal. The only thing he hasn't turned over to me is you. You're his wife, after all!* ***How could I violate his trust and sin against God?***" *She pestered him day after day after day, but he stood his ground. He refused to go to bed with her. On one of these days he came to the house to do his work and none of the household servants happened to be there. She grabbed him by his cloak, saying, "Sleep with me!" He left his coat in her hand and ran out of the house.*[17]

If Joseph could run from sin because he had a knowledge of his closeness to God in the Old Testament, you and I can do better under the New Testament if we consciously allow our minds to focus on our proximity to God. This understanding enables us to think and act in a special manner because of a truth, we are!

Some people lack this understanding that is why they are often carried away by sinful pleasures. They usually think that God is far away. Paul addressed this issue in the Corinthian Church. He emphasized that the major cause of their moral failures was simply that they lacked the knowledge of their proximity to and connection with God.

> *Awake [from your drunken stupor and return] to sober sense and your right minds, and sin no more.* ***For some of you have not the knowledge of God [you are utterly***

and willfully and disgracefully ignorant, and continue to be so, lacking the sense of God's presence and all true knowledge of Him]. I say this to your shame.[18]

Do you not discern and understand that you [the whole church at Corinth] are God's temple (His sanctuary), and that God's Spirit has His permanent dwelling in you [to be at home in you, collectively as a church and also individually]?[19]

Don't become partners with those who reject God. How can you make a partnership out of right and wrong? That's not partnership; that's war. Is light best friend with dark? Does Christ go strolling with the Devil? Do trust and mistrust hold hands? Who would think of setting up pagan idols in God's holy Temple? ***But that is exactly what we are, each of us a temple in whom God lives. God himself put it this way: "I'll live in them, move into them; I'll be their God and they'll be my people****. So leave the corruption and compromise; leave it for good," says God. "Don't link up with those who will pollute you.* ***I want you all for myself. I'll be a Father to you; you'll be sons and daughters to me." The Word of the Master, God****."*[20]

"Your proximity and connection to God doesn't give you the liberty and motivation to enjoy sin. Rather, it gives you capacity to resist and reject sin." – **RSD**

The essence of all these insightful information is for you to realize that you are very special because you were created in God's image and likeness. You have the attitude of God and the attributes of God. God wants to walk with you, for you, through you and in you. You are so special that He actually wants to live with you and loves to dwell in you. So, don't ever allow the devil, economic conditions, people's opinions or comments, self-condemnation and negative situations define or discourage you. Don't also allow the pleasures of sin to distract you from God because those pleasures are actually temporal and the devil merely uses them as a bait to destroy your relationship with God so that he can utterly destroy you too.

"Never allow any sinful behavior affect your proximity to God because you are a special gem with royalty and eternal dignity in totality." – **RSD**

"You are very special because you have God's identity, capacity, ability, authority and you are His utmost priority." – **RSD**

What were your key learning points from this chapter?

What are the new things you will do or actions you will take with these lessons?

PRODUCTIVITY

"God made you special because of the special task and assignment He wants you to accomplish for Him in the world." RSD

Before I made you in your mother's womb, I knew you. Before you were born, I chose you for a ***SPECIAL WORK***[21a]

A man from the family of Levi married a Levite woman. The woman became pregnant and had a son. She saw there was ***something SPECIAL about him and hid him. She hid him for three months.*** *When she couldn't hide him any longer she got a little basket-boat made of papyrus, waterproofed it with tar and pitch, and placed the child in it. Then she set it afloat in the reeds at the edge of the Nile. The baby's older sister found herself a vantage point a little way off and watched to see what would happen to him. Pharaoh's daughter came down to the Nile to bathe; her maidens strolled on the bank. She saw the basket-boat floating in the reeds and sent her maid to get it. She opened it and saw the child a baby crying! Her heart went out to*

> *him. She said, "This must be one of the Hebrew babies." Then his sister was before her: "Do you want me to go and get a nursing mother from the Hebrews so she can nurse the baby for you?" Pharaoh's daughter said, "Yes. Go." The girl went and called the child's mother. Pharaoh's daughter told her, "Take this baby and nurse him for me. I'll pay you." The woman took the child and nursed him. After the child was weaned, she presented him to Pharaoh's daughter who adopted him as her son. She named him Moses (Pulled-Out), saying, "I pulled him out of the water."*[21b]

In concluding these phenomenal principles about your peculiarity as an individual, it is important to note that God has a special purpose and assignment that He wants you to accomplish. That is why He made you so special and unique with different gifts, talents and abilities that will enable you accomplish that task. The mother of Moses noticed that he was a special child. Moses had a unique assignment on earth. Thanks to God that he was very conscious of it even though he was raised by the daughter of Pharaoh, the Egyptian king. He was not satisfied with the comforts of the palace. He knew that there was more to his life than just some temporary comfort. He made an attempt to deliver the children of Israel without an appropriate strategy and failed. And even when he escaped from Egypt to Midian, he continued to live a very productive life. At one time, he rescued some ladies from molesters and also watered their sheep. In fact, his divine encounter with God and his divine mandate to deliver the Israelites from their long years of bondage in Egypt came while he was being productive. The bible records it thus:

> *The priest of Midian had seven daughters. They came and drew water, filling the troughs and watering their father's sheep. When some shepherds came and chased the girls off,* ***Moses came to their rescue and helped them water their sheep.***
>
> ***Moses was shepherding the flock of Jethro****, his father-in-law, the priest of Midian. He led the flock to the west end of the wilderness and came to the mountain of God, Horeb. The angel of God appeared to him in flames of fire blazing out of the middle of a bush. He looked. The bush was blazing away but it didn't burn up. Moses said, "What's going on here? I can't believe this! Amazing! Why doesn't the bush burn up?" God saw that he had stopped to look. God called to him from out of the bush, "Moses! Moses!" He said, "Yes? I'm right here!" God said, "Don't come any closer. Remove your sandals from your feet. You're standing on holy ground." Then he said, "I am the God of your father: The God of Abraham, the God of Isaac, and the God of Jacob." Moses hid his face, afraid to look at God. God said, "I've taken a good, long look at the affliction of my people in Egypt. I've heard their cries for deliverance from their slave masters; I know all about their pain. And now I have come down to help them, pry them loose from the grip of Egypt, get them out of that country and bring them to a*

> *good land with wide-open spaces, a land lush with milk and honey, the land of the Canaanite, the Hittite, the Amorite, the Perizzite, the Hivite, and the Jebusite. "The Israelite cry for help has come to me, and I've seen for myself how cruelly they're being treated by the Egyptians.* ***It's time for you to go back: I'm sending you to Pharaoh to bring my people, the People of Israel, out of Egypt." Moses answered God, "But why me? What makes you think that I could ever go to Pharaoh and lead the children of Israel out of Egypt?" "I'll be with you," God said. "And this will be the proof that I am the one who sent you: When you have brought my people out of Egypt, you will worship God right here at this very mountain."***[22]

Productivity is the quality, state, or fact of being able to generate, create, enhance, or bring forth goods and services. It means thriving, flourishing, inventive, creative and fruitful. Moses was so productive and proactive that he not only delivered the children of Israel by carefully following God's instructions, he diligently documented the whole process. Moses, due to his productivity, was able to patiently, carefully and accurately document the story and revelation of creation and all the events that happened several years before he was born. Have you ever thought about the fact that all the stories in Genesis were written by someone who wasn't around when it happened? You also have a special assignment that God wants you to bless humanity with. Can you imagine if Moses had not written Genesis, Exodus, Leviticus, Numbers and Deuteronomy? There are several ideas, inventions, products and services that will bring solutions to some of the problems in our world that are yet to come from you.

The fact that you are special means that sometimes you will also experience some special challenges that may want to hinder the fulfillment of your dreams, visions, purposes and assignments in life. Such challenges may be in your health, family or relationships, finances, economy, education, nation and so on just like it happened to Joseph. He was a special child with special problem from his family. He was hated by his brothers, threatened with death and was eventually sold as a slave into another country where he was falsely accused of attempted rape and imprisoned for years. The good thing about Joseph was that because he knew that he was a very special individual with a special assignment on earth, he didn't allow all those challenges to stop his productivity. This was why he kept serving from his home, in slavery and in the prison till his productivity took him to the palace as the prime minister of Egypt. Even after his promotion, he remained productive. This account validates his value for work.

> *Joseph [who had been in Egypt thirteen years] was thirty years old when he stood before Pharaoh king of Egypt.*

> ***Joseph went out from the presence of Pharaoh and went [about his DUTIES] through all the land of Egypt****. In the seven abundant years the earth brought forth by handfuls [for each seed planted]. And he gathered up all the [surplus] food of the seven [good] years in the land of Egypt and stored up the food in the cities; he stored away in each city the food from the fields around it. And Joseph gathered grain as the sand of the sea, very much, until he stopped counting, for it could not be measured.*[23]

"When you have a good mentality of your specialty and the peculiarity of your assignment, you won't allow any difficulty to hinder your productivity" – **RSD**

You need to understand that you are special and different from others because of God's deposits in you and His assignment for you. Hence, nothing and no one should make you feel inferior in anyway. No situation should make you feel depressed. No devil and no demonic power is strong enough to suppress or oppress you because God is not only in you, with you and for you but also walks with you and works for you so you can truly experience all the benefits of redemption and express the ultimate reason for your creation.

Paul the apostle enjoyed special grace from God simply because of his special assignment on earth. He said that:

> *But by the grace (the unmerited favor and blessing) of God I am what I am, and His grace toward me was not [found*

> *to be] for nothing (fruitless and without effect). In fact, I WORKED harder than all of them [the apostles], though it was not really I, but the grace (the unmerited favor and blessing) of God which was with me.*[24]

Peter who was the head of the disciples, leader of the church and a direct trainee of Jesus never envied Paul and didn't express any bitterness over the success of his ministry. In spite of the fact that Paul did not have the opportunity to be trained directly by Jesus, he had results that far outweighed that of the other apostles. Rather than envy Paul because of his unfathomable results, Peter acknowledged that God gave Paul unusual wisdom and insight:

> *Don't forget that the Lord is patient because he wants people to be saved. This is also what our dear friend Paul said when he wrote you with the wisdom that God had given him.*[25]

You don't need to compete with anyone, compare yourself with anyone, complain about anyone, condemn yourself or anyone because of their works, successes or who they are. Instead, learn to compliment others while you focus on fulfilling your own purpose and completing your task and assignment in life. Always live in the consciousness that as a child of God, created in His image (His unique attributes and attitudes) and in His likeness, you have extraordinary features that would ensure you enjoy a colorful, blissful, fruitful and wonderful future as a result of the fact that:

"You are special because of your exceptional Personality, Peculiarity, Posterity, Prosperity, Possibility mentality, Propensity and Proximity to God which are all given to you for outstanding Productivity and the good of humanity." – **RSD**

Your old identity of failure, fear, faithlessness, frustration, fruitlessness, struggles, stagnation, strain, stress, sickness and sin are all gone the moment you allow Jesus to become the savior of your life and the standard for your personality. Whatever cannot defeat Jesus cannot defeat you. You are now a special individual because you are connected to the most Supreme Being in the universe. Allow this truth to guide how you see yourself always like the Apostle Paul did in the scripture. This understanding empowered him for extraordinary feats and accomplishments in spite of his negative past. He described his new identity in this manner:

> *"My old identity has been co-crucified with Messiah and no longer lives; for the nails of his cross crucified me with him. And now the essence of this new life is no longer mine, for the Anointed One lives his life through me—we live in union as one! My new life is empowered by the faith of the Son of God who loves me so much that he gave himself for me, and dispenses his life into mine!*[26]

What were your key learning points from this chapter?

What are the new things you will do or actions you will take with these lessons?

TAKE ACTION

I believe the journey through this book has been both inspirational and impactful for you. However, the best way to maximize the wealth of knowledge in this piece is to make a solid decision about your relationship with God by taking advantage of the grace for forgiveness and freedom from the debts of sin which He offers. You and I owe a debt of sin which we cannot pay because of our limitations but that debt has been paid by Jesus Christ. All we need to do is to take a step of faith and receive God's free gift of salvation.

If you would like to embark on this life-transforming journey today, kindly say the prayer below:

Lord Jesus, I accept you today as my Lord and saviour. I receive forgiveness for all my sins through your blood that was shed for me and I declare today that I am a child of God. I receive your grace to finish my race in life with great testimonies because I am really and truly special.

Thank you Lord.

PLEASE SHARE THE TESTIMONIES OF THE IMPACT THIS BOOK HAS HAD ON YOU

Send the testimonies of your experience with this book and the impacts it has had on you to these email addresses:

wowglobals@gmail.com,
ralphsegundada@gmail.com

Someone will be encouraged by your testimony.

You can also send an SMS to +2348075170325

SPECIAL APPRECIATION

There is no self-made man. I deeply appreciate Yetunde Macaulay, Aderonke Adeniran and Kingsley Obom-Egbulem for working on the manuscripts to make it suitable for publication. My sincere gratitude to Samuel Awoma for the excellent graphic design and to everyone that contributed in various ways to the success of this book. You are indeed very special.

Special thanks and appreciation to all who have sent in their testimonies and praise reports to us about the impacts this book has had on them. Kindly note that all testimonies are received in good faith and edited only for brevity and fluency. Names have been changed to protect the writers' privacy.

BOOK NOTES

1. Exodus 19:6 *(The Message Bible)*

2. a.Mathew19:27-29 (The Living Bible),
   b. http://www.personalitypage.com/html/high-level.html,
   c. Psalm 139:13-14, ERV, (Easy to Read Version) NCV (New Century Version), YLT (Young Literal Translations)
   d. 1Corinthians 10:12 NIV, MSG, AMP (Amplified Bible Classic Edition),
   e. 1Peter2:9 *(The Amplified Bible)*

3. a. Gen 1:26 *(The Living Bible),*
   b. Acts 7:9 AMP,
   c. Genesis 49:26 NASBU (New Amereican Standard Bible Updated Edition)

4. a. Psalm 92:13-14 NJKV, TLB, AMPC,
   b. Isaiah 8: 18 *(Bible in Basic English)*

5. a. Genesis 39: 2 AMP,
   b. Genesis 1:28 *(The Message Bible)*
   c. 3John 2 NKJV

6. a. Genesis 11:6,
   b. Acts 10:38 *(The Easy to Read Bible)*

7. a. Philippians 2: 5 *(The King James Bible),* 1 Corinthians 2:16 AMP.

8. 1 John 3:1 *(The Message Bible)*

9. Jeremiah 31:2-3 *(The Message Bible)*

10. Luke 15:11-32 *(The Message Bible)*

11. a. Luke 3:22,
    b. Mathew 6: 5-9,
    c. *Isaiah 49:14-16, 63:16 (The Message Bible),*
    d. Ephesians 3:14-20 AMP.
    e. 2 Corinthians 11:23-29 TLB,
    f. Romans 8:35-39,
    g. John 13:23 AMP.
    h. 1John 2:15-16 NKJV,
    i. John 3:16 AMP,
    j. Romans 5:8 AMP.
    k. 1 John 4:16-19 AMP.
    l. Luke 3:21-22, 4:2-3 (The Message Bible)

m. Daniel 10:11, 12, 19 AMP,
n. Jude 21AMP.
o. Psalm 23: 6 AMP.

12. *Ephesians 2:1-13. (New Century Version).*

13. *Genesis 3:8-11. (Amplified).*

14. *Hebrews 9:24-26 (Amplified)*

15. *Hebrews 4:14-16 (Amplified)*

16. *Mathew 27:46, 51-53 (The Living Bible)*

17. *Genesis 39:6-14 (Message Bible)*

18. *1 Corinthians 15:34 (Amplified)*

19. *1 Corinthians 3:16 (Amplified)*

20. *2 Corinthians 6:14-18 (Amplified)*

21a. Jeremiah 1:5 ERV (Easy to Read Version)
21b. Exodus 2:16-17 Message Translation

22. Exodus 3:1-12 Message Translation

23. Genesis 41:46-49 AMP (Amplified)

24. 1 Corinthians 15:10 AMPC (Amplified Bible Classic Edition)

25. 2 Peter 3:15 CEV (Contemporary English Version)

26. Galatians 2:20 TPT (The Passion Translation)

Let the wise hear and increase in learning, and the one who understands obtain guidance
~ Proverb 1:5 .ESV

"Your lifetime earnings will increase proportionate to your learning and your yearning for God" **RSD**.

Visit: www.ralphsegundada.com

To download all Pastor Ralph Audio Messages for free on the audio library.

Enjoy inspiring articles that will transform your life and also motivate you to fulfill your purpose, dreams and goals in life.

THE AUTHOR

Ralph Segun Dada (RSD) is an assiduous development enthusiast and a leadership expert. He has a divine mandate to teach Purpose and Fulfillment principles drawing inspiration from the Word of God. Ralph is a gifted, graced and proficient teacher, trainer, mentor and motivator.

He has successfully undergone several personal development and leadership programs from prestigious institutions including Lagos Business School (LBS), Daystar Leadership Academy and Word of Faith Bible Institute. He holds a Bachelor's degree in Accountancy.

Ralph is an Associate Pastor at Daystar Christian Centre in Lagos Nigeria where he serves in various capacities as faculty member and facilitator at the Daystar Leadership Academy with specialization in Leadership, Leadership Development, Entrepreneurship, Dynamics of Vision, Delegation Strategies, Financial Management, and Excellence Oriented Organization among many others. He pioneered Daystar Alimosho/Egbeda Satellite Centre, a very fast-growing church with outstanding growth that runs 3 powerful services within one and half years of inauguration.

Before Ralph became a full-time pastor, he has effectively and efficiently led the marketing, training and customer service departments in the corporate world as a strategist and growth booster with an excellent dimension to team building.

He is also the president of Ralph Segun Dada Foundation established to Restore, Support and Develop lives in various capacities and with a special focus on the transformation of the younger generation. Ralph is an author, conference speaker and passionate about music.

www.ralphsegundada.com

Follow Ralph Segun Dada on all Social Media Platforms @rsegundada

Subscribe to Ralph Segun Dada RSDTV On Youtube

OTHER BOOKS BY THE AUTHOR

The book contains insightful and intensive information that would greatly impact the reader.

It intends to:

- Erase doubts about the possibilities of enjoying maximum fulfillment in life.
- Give every reader access to relevant, tested and proven principles on how to attain maximum fulfillment.
- Illustrate in details the various reasons why one needs to be totally fulfilled in life.

Reading this book and diligently making the principles in it a way of life will give each reader the motivation, inspiration and empowerment to enjoy maximum fulfillment in all areas of life regardless of life's challenges. It is a book that must be gotten for yourself and other people and should be read over and over again. It is really a manual, compendium, treatise and guide for Maximum Fulfillment.

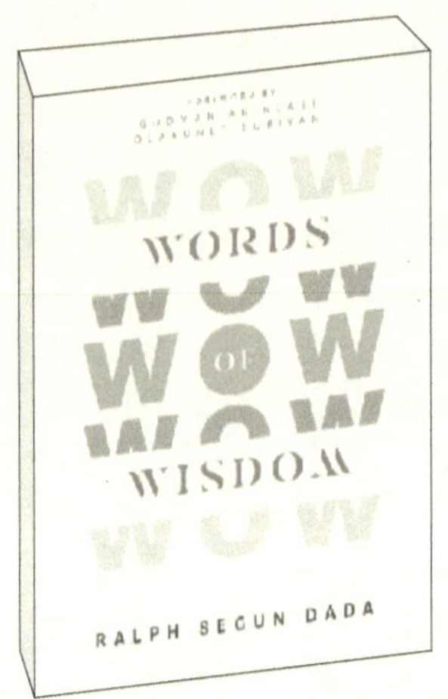

This book is inspired to produce an invaluable, positive change in your life. It contains 1,500 scripture-based FRESH AND ORIGINAL, thrilling, timely and relevant quotations and words of inspiration which cover virtually all areas of life. It is an absolute necessity for every preacher, counselor, teacher, writer, motivational speaker and all that desire to communicate with impact either publicly or privately. It can also serve as booster to daily devotions. Reading it will give you the right perspective to the following:

- Vision, Ambition, Purpose, Potential, Choice, Desire, Direction, Determination and Good decision making.
- Attitude, Character, Habits formation, Focus, Discipline and Self-control
- Reading, Studying, Personal development, Planning, Management, Preparation, Investment, Goal setting
- Action, Diligence, Persistence, Commitment, Thought, Imagination and the Value of meditation
- Christian growth, Maturity, Leadership, Faith, Heaven, Purity and many more.

www.ingramcontent.com/pod-product-compliance
Lightning Source LLC
LaVergne TN
LVHW091025150826
845672LV00006BA/1685
9789789570140